GOD
IN OUR MIDST

Seeking and Receiving
Ongoing Revival

James I. Packer

GOD
IN OUR MIDST

Seeking and Receiving
Ongoing Revival

WORD PUBLISHING

Word (UK) Ltd
Milton Keynes, England

WORD BOOKS AUSTRALIA
Heathmont, Victoria, Australia

SUNDAY SCHOOL CENTRE WHOLESALE
Salt River, South Africa

ALBY COMMERCIAL ENTERPRISES PTE LTD
Scotts Road, Singapore

CONCORDE DISTRIBUTORS LTD
Havelock North, New Zealand

CROSS (HK) CO
Hong Kong

PRAISE INC
Quezon City, Philippines

GOD IN OUR MIDST

Copyright © 1987 by James I. Packer.

First published in the USA by Servant Publications.

God in Our Midst is based on James I. Packer, "Steps to the Renewal of the Christian People," *Summons to Faith and Renewal* (Ann Arbor, Michigan: Servant Books, 1983).

First UK Edition 1987.

ISBN 0–85009–135–7 (Australia 1–86258–033–2)

Reproduced, printed and bound in Great Britain for Word (UK) Ltd., by Cox & Wyman Ltd., Reading.

THE TASK AND THE METHOD

In the following pages I address myself to a twofold task: first, to formulate a clear view of what the renewal of the church really is, and then to say what needs to happen in order to get us there, starting from where we are. And in tackling that twofold task I have a twofold goal: to speak both to your minds and to your hearts. For I shall try, not just to state God's truth, but also to apply it by way of challenging your concern and your action.

Who am I, you may ask, to set myself this agenda? Let me tell you. I am an expatriate Englishman, an Episcopal pastor by calling and a Reformed theologian by trade, who in 1945, soon after his conversion, was given a copy of Charles G. Finney's *Lectures on Revivals of Religion* (1835), and who since that time has carried a personal burden of concern for the renewing of God's people through a fresh outpouring of the Holy Spirit. On this subject I have spoken repeatedly, written occasionally, and thought constantly throughout those years. Now I seek to enlist you for the pursuit of the same interest, and I am grateful for the opportunity to do so.

There is, however, one thing that I need to say at the very outset about the manner of pursuing an interest of this kind. Renewal in all its aspects is not a theme for dilettante debate, but for humble, penitent, prayerful, faith-full exploration before the Lord, with a willingness to change and be changed, and if necessary to be the first to be changed, if that is what the truth proves to require. To absorb ideas about renewal ordinarily costs nothing, but to enter into renewal could cost us everything we have, and we shall be very guilty if, having come to understand renewal, we then decline it. We need to be clear about that. John Calvin once declared that it would be better for a preacher to break his neck while mounting the pulpit if he did not himself intend to be the first to follow God.[1] In the same way, it would be better for us not to touch the study of renewal at all if we are not ourselves ready to be the first to be renewed. I speak as to wise men; please judge what I say.

By what method, now, shall we approach our subject? Here the gates of two "by-path meadows," to use Bunyan's phrase, stand invitingly open. First, it is tempting to come at the renewal theme *sociologically*. That would mean defining "the Christian people" in external and institutional terms, as an organized association with specific goals; equating renewal with the achieving of those goals; and then occupying ourselves in pragmatic reflection on what structural and attitudinal changes would have to be engineered in order to realize these goals in a statistically measurable way. The idea that the church's health problems can be solved by such manipulation is not unfamiliar, at least to members of major Protestant denominations in North America; analysts both inside and outside denominational headquarters do a great deal of thinking at this level. Nor do I dismiss such analysis as useless; on the contrary, it does much to make us aware of lacks and needs in the church's life. But I urge most emphatically that the renewal of the church is in essence a spiritual and supernatural matter, a work of the Holy Spirit enriching our fellowship with the Father and the Son, and it takes more than clever social engineering to bring this about.

Again, it is tempting to come at our theme *historically*. That would mean identifying past movements of renewal and revival, from the Old Testament records of Israel's return to Yahweh under Asa, Hezekiah, Josiah, Ezra, and others, and the New Testament story in Acts of revival in Palestine after Pentecost, through to the Cistercian and Dominican and Franciscan movements; the ministry of Savonarola; the Western Reformation; the early Jesuits; English Puritanism and Lutheran Pietism; the Evangelical Awakenings in old England and New England in the eighteenth century; the repeated stirrings of the

Spirit in Wales and Scotland between the seventeenth and nineteenth centuries; the first hundred years of the Protestant missionary movement; the frontier revivals in America; the worldwide quickenings among Protestants in the 1850s and again in the 1900s; the East African revival, now fifty years old and still continuing; the awakenings in Lewis, off the west coast of Scotland, in the 1950s, in Western Canada in the 1960s, and in Indonesia and the Californian "Jesus movement" in the 1970s; the impact of the worldwide charismatic movement over the past twenty years; and so on. It would then mean analyzing, comparing, reconstructing, and characterizing these movements in the way that historians do, and seeking to produce out of this exercise generalized typologies of renewal for future reference. Now I do not wish to minimize the very great value of this kind of study. The psalmists charge us to keep God's mighty works in remembrance, and we should be glad that in our day so much printed material on past renewal movements is available to us.[2] But if all we did was study renewal historically, we should in the first place be looking at it in a merely external and this-worldly way, as the phenomenon of changed outlooks and activities in certain persons' lives. And in the second place we could hardly avoid lapsing into what I call the antiquarian fallacy about renewal, the assumption that any future renewal will become recognizable by conforming to some pattern set in the past. That there are such patterns is not in doubt; they merit careful examination, and in that connection I commend in particular Richard Lovelace's pioneer theological phenomenology of renewal, *Dynamics of Spiritual Life* (1979). But we should limit God improperly, and actually quench the Spirit, if we assumed that future movements of renewal will correspond in outward form to some past movement, and that we can rely on this correspondence as a means of identifying them. Renewal is precisely God doing a new thing, and though every work of renewal has basic qualities, or dimensions, in common with every other, we must recognize that the contours of the cultures within which the church has from time to time lost its vitality, and also the contours of that loss in itself, have varied; which means that it is not safe for us to assume that the outward forms and phenomena of revival in this or any future age will always prove to have exact historical precedents. At this point sad mistakes in judgment have been made in the past, and I suspect are being made by some in the present. Let us strive not to be of their number.

What I have said makes it apparent, I hope, that our basic need in studying renewal is for categories and criteria that are neither sociological nor historical but theological, which for me at least means biblically based. With Scripture as our guide, therefore, we shall now discuss, first, the *theology* of renewal (that is, the overall account that should be given of renewal as a work of God); second, the *elements* in renewal (that is, specific things that occur when this work of God is in progress); third, the *quest* for renewal (that is, the steps in seeking renewal which we and the segments of the body of Christ to which we belong could take, starting now).

The Theology of Renewal

For some decades the word "renewal" has been used loosely in the world church, with applications as wide as they are unfocused. The general sense that renewal is needed because the church is not all that it should be is welcome, but the vague way in which the word is thrown around is unhelpful, to say the least. Contemporary voices celebrate liturgical renewal, theological renewal, lay renewal, ecumenical renewal, charismatic renewal, and renewal in other departments too; indeed, it seems that any new outburst of activity in the church, any cloud of dust raised by the stamping of excited feet, will be hailed as renewal by somebody. Certainly, there is no renewal without activity, and when renewal is a reality every area of the church's life should benefit. But the implicit equating of renewal with enthusiasm and activity is inadequate in two ways. First, it gives an idea of renewal which is far too *inclusive:* horizontally, so to speak, it embraces too much. For in biblical thought and experience, renewal is linked with divine visitation, purging judgment, and restoration through repentance, and no amount of hustle and bustle qualifies as renewal where these notes are absent. Second, this equation gives an idea of renewal which is far too *superficial:* vertically, so to speak, it does not include enough. It views renewal in terms of externals only, and takes no account of the inward exercise of heart in encounter with God in which true renewal as Scripture depicts it always begins. But hustle and bustle do not constitute renewal apart from this inward dimension.

How then should we define renewal? The word is one of a group—spiritual, renewal, revival, awakening, visitation, reformation—which tend to be used together and need to be defined together. Five of these six are correlated by Richard Lovelace in a way which both corresponds to usage and clarifies the realities involved. I quote him, *"Spiritual* (as in *spiritual life, spiritual gifts*) . . . means *deriving from the Holy Spirit,* which is its normal significance in scripture. *Renewal, revival,* and *awakening* trace back to biblical metaphors for the infusion of spiritual life in Christian experience by the Holy Spirit (see Rom 6:4, 8:2-11; Eph 1:17-23, 3:14-19, 5:14). Usually they are used synonymously for broad-scale movements of the Holy Spirit's work in renewing spiritual vitality in the church and in fostering its expansion in mission and evangelism. *Reformation* refers to the purifying of doctrine and structures in the church, but implies also a component of spiritual revitalization. *Renewal* is sometimes used to encompass revival and reformation, and also to include *aggiornamento,* the updating of the church leading to a new engagement with the surrounding world."[3] To Lovelace's definitions I add that *visitation,* the sixth word in the group, signifies the initial divine approach to spiritually moribund communities out of which their renewal comes.

Lovelace's two definitions of *renewal* alert us to the fact that this is one of those "concertina-words" which in use keep alternating between a narrower and a broader significance. The term carries its narrowest meaning (concertina closed) when it is used of the personal quickening of an individual. Used so, it signifies that his spiritual life—that is, his God-given fellowship with the Father and the Son through the Spirit, the saving relationship which finds expression in his praise and prayer, his devotion and character, his work and his witness—has been decisively deepened through God's visiting his soul. ("His," by the way, in that last sentence includes "hers"; I am not suggesting that only males experience personal renewal!) At the other end of the scale, *renewal* has its broadest meaning (concertina open) when it is applied to the church, for here, in idea at any rate, it signifies revitalizing at every level, starting with believers' inner lives (what Puritans called their "heart-work") and extending to all the characteristic public activities in which the body of Christ is called to engage. I will focus on the latter, broader application of the word. You cannot, of course, have corporate renewal of any part of the body of Christ on earth without personal renewal of those who make it up, although the quickening of individuals can and does constantly occur without it being part of any larger local movement; but here I shall speak of personal renewal only in the context of corporate renewal, the quickening of "the Christian people" in this place or that.

In terms of biblical theology, now, we can characterize God's work of renewal in the following three ways.

First, renewal is an *eschatological* reality, in the sense that it is a general experiential deepening of that life in the Spirit which is the foretaste and first installment of heaven itself. Assurance of both the shameful guiltiness and the total pardon of our sins; joy, humble but exalted, in the awareness of God's love for us; knowledge of the closeness of the Father and the Son in both communion and affection; a never-ending passion to praise God; an abiding urge to love, serve, and honor the Father, the Son, the Spirit, and the saints, and inward freedom to express that urge creatively and spontaneously—these things will be the essence of the life of heaven, and they are already the leading marks of spiritually renewed individuals and communities in this world. To describe situations of renewal, as Protestants using the word *revival* are prone to do, as heaven on earth is not devotional hyperbole; intrinsically and ontologically, that is exactly what the renewal of the Christian people is.

Second, renewal is a *Christological* reality, in two ways. First, it is *subjectively* Christocentric, in the sense that awareness of the gracious, beneficent personal presence of the glorified Lord Jesus—"Jesus, my Shepherd, Husband, Friend, my Prophet, Priest and King, my Lord, my life, my way, my end," as Newton's marvelous hymn puts it; Jesus, who guards, guides, keeps, and feeds me, and finally receives me to be with him forever, in glory—is the very heart of the renewed Christian's sense of reality. The vision of Christ's glory, the realization that every one of

God's good gifts comes to us through him and the passion to love and adore him, come to pervade the minds and hearts of persons in renewal to a degree that is a major anticipation of heaven, as was said in the last paragraph. The lady who explained to me her identification with a certain renewal movement by saying, "I just want the Lord Jesus to run my life," could not have been better directed: she was after the right thing, and she was looking for it in the right place. It is precisely in renewal that love of Jesus and fellowship with him become most clear-sighted and deep. The most obvious evidence of this is the hymnology of renewal movements. Charles Wesley was the supreme poet of love to Jesus in a revival context: think of his "Jesus, lover of my soul," and the final stanzas of "Thou hidden source of calm repose"—

> Jesus, my all in all thou art,
>   My rest in toil, my ease in pain,
> The medicine of my broken heart,
>   In war my peace, in loss my gain,
> My smile beneath the tyrant's frown,
>   In shame my glory and my crown;
> In want my plentiful supply,

In weakness my almighty power,
In bonds my perfect liberty,
    My light in Satan's darkest hour,
In grief my joy unspeakable,
    My life in death, my heaven in hell.

Or think of this, from the supreme preacher of love to Christ in a renewal context, Bernard of Clairvaux:

Jesus, the very thought of thee
    With sweetness fills my breast;
But sweeter far thy face to see,
    And in thy presence rest.
O hope of every contrite heart,
    O joy of all the meek,
To those who fall how kind thou art!
    How good to those who seek!
But what to those who find? Ah! this
    Nor tongue nor pen can show:
The love of Jesus, what it is,
    None but his loved ones know.
Jesus, our only joy be thou,
    As thou our prize wilt be;
Jesus, be thou our glory now
    And through eternity.

One mark of spiritual authenticity in the renewal songs of our time—Christian camp fire songs, as they have sometimes been called—is that in them the theme of Christ's love for us and ours for him surfaces once more, and strongly.

Second, renewal is *objectively* Christocentric, in the sense that through it believers are drawn deeper into their baptismal life of dying with Christ in repentance and self-denial and rising with him into the new righteousness of combating sin and living in obedience to God. Authentic revivals have deep ethical effects; they produce authentic sanctity— really, though not always uniformly, tidily, or calmly—along with authentic ministry one to another; and both these features of authentic Christianity should be viewed as the supernatural life of Christ himself living and serving in and through his members by means of the operation of the Spirit. Also, the intensified communion with Christ should be seen as based upon the dynamic reality of this our union with him—or, better, this his union with us.

The third point in the biblical concept of renewal is that it is a *pneumatological* reality, in the sense that it is through the action of the Holy Spirit doing his New Covenant work of glorifying the glorified Christ before the eyes of the understanding of his disciples, in the manner described above, that renewal actually takes place. Here, incidentally, is a sure test of whether particular stirrings of excitement about interior experience of God are instances of Holy Spirit renewal or not: as Jonathan Edwards argued against critics of the Great Awakening, it is not the devil who exalts Christ, but the Holy Spirit, so that if the experiences in question deepen Christ-centered devotion, that proves their source. And if they do not, that proves their source too. For Satan's strategy is always to distract men from Christ, and getting them to concentrate on exotic experiences—visions, voices, thrills, drug trips, and all the mumbo-jumbo of false mysticism and nonrational meditation—is as good a way for him to do it as any other.

In addition to characterizing renewal in this way, biblical theology answers for us the question, what place has renewal in God's overall purposes? "Restore us again, O God of our salvation," prays the psalmist, "and put away thy indignation toward us! Wilt thou be angry with us for ever? Wilt thou prolong thy anger to all generations? Wilt thou not revive us again, that thy people may rejoice in thee?" (Ps 85:4-6). Those verses, which can be matched from many passages in the psalms and the prophets, beg for a quickening visitation to the community ("restore, or revive, *us* again") which will have a twofold experiential significance. First, this reviving will be experienced as *the ending of God's wrath,* the termination of the impotence, frustration, and barrenness which have been the tokens of divine displeasure for unfaithfulness. Second, this reviving will be experienced as *the exulting of God's people:* joy will replace the distress which knowledge of God's displeasure has made the faithful feel. Then, third, as appears most clearly from the Acts narrative, such reviving is also experienced as *the extending of God's kingdom.* God's visitation to renew his own household regularly has an evangelistic and cultural overflow, often of great power, leading to the fulfillment in churchly terms of what Zechariah foresaw in terms of the post-exilic restoration: "Ten men from the nations of every tongue shall take hold of the robe of the Jew, saying, 'Let us go with you, for we have heard that God is with you'" (Zech 8:23). Again and again, for the glory of God in and through his church, this pattern of events has needed to recur, and has in fact recurred, both in and since the biblical period.

In *Dynamics of Spiritual Life,* Dr. Lovelace argues that the apparent antithesis between the two models of cyclical and continuous renewal which the Old and New Testaments respectively seem to throw up is not absolute since the same spiritual forces operate in both types of situations.[4] I agree, and to clarify the point I offer a distinction between *renewing* or *reviving* as an act of God— that is, the initial visitation which sparks off a new movement—and *revival* or *renewal* itself—that is, the state of revivedness in which God's people continue until for whatever cause the power of the original visitation is withdrawn. Thus one may say that

Pentecost was a day of renewing; that renewal conditions surrounded all the protagonists of the church history recorded in Acts, as the New Testament letters also show by the quality of the devotional experience to which they testify; but that six of the seven churches of the Apocalypse had quenched the Spirit, so that the quality of their inward responsiveness to Jesus Christ was now noticeably reduced, and repentance on their part and a fresh visitation from their Lord was urgently needed. How this might bear on the present life of our own churches, and on our own roles and responsibilities within them, is something at which we must look with some care. But first we should spend a moment reviewing the *elements* in revival, which I announced as the second part of our discussion.

The Elements in Renewal

The phenomena of renewal movements merit much more study by church historians, theologians, and exponents of

Christian spirituality than they have yet received. At surface level, they vary widely, as do the movements within which they appear, and we should not be surprised at that. For, in the first place, spiritual movements are partly shaped by preexisting needs, which in their turn reflect all sorts of nonrecurring cultural and economic factors, as well as many aspects of the morbid pathology of sin and spiritual decline; and, in the second place, the spiritual experiences of Christians are determined in part by temperament, by atmosphere, and by pressure groups, all of which are variables; and, in the third place, God the Lord appears to delight in variety and never quite repeats himself. But at the level of deeper analysis, deeper, that is, than verbal and cultural variants and preset interpretative grids, there are constant factors recognizable in all biblical and post-biblical revivals and renewals of faith and life, whatever their historical, racial, and cultural settings. They number five, as follows: awareness of God's presence; responsiveness to

God's word; sensitiveness to sin; liveliness in community; fruitfulness in testimony. Let me illustrate them briefly.

(1) Awareness of God's presence. The first and fundamental feature in renewal is the sense that God has drawn awesomely near in his holiness, mercy, and might. This is felt as the fulfilling of the prayer of Isaiah 64:1f: "O that thou would rend the heavens and come down, that the mountains might quake at thy presence . . . to make thy name known to thine adversaries, and that the nations may tremble at thy presence." God "comes," "visits" his people, and makes his majesty known. The effect is the same as it was for Isaiah himself, when he "saw the Lord sitting on a throne" in the temple and heard the angels' song—"Holy, holy, holy"—and was forced to cry, "Woe is me, for I am ruined! Because I am a man of unclean lips, and I live among a people of unclean lips" (Is 6:1-5). It is with this searching, scorching manifestation of God's presence that renewal begins, and by its continuance that renewal is sustained. Says Arthur

Wallis: "The spirit of revival is the consciousness of God."[5] Wrote Duncan Campbell, out of his experience of revival in Lewis from 1949 to 1953: "I have no hesitation in saying that this awareness of God is the crying need of the church today."[6] This, and nothing less than this, is what the outpouring of the Spirit in renewal means in experiential terms.

(2)Responsiveness to God's word. The sense of God's presence imparts new authority to his truth. The message of Scripture which previously was making only a superficial impact, if that, now searches its hearers and readers to the depth of their being. The statement that "the word of God is living and active, sharper than any two-edged sword, piercing to the division of soul and spirit, of joints and marrow, and discerning the thoughts and intentions of the heart" (Heb 4:12) is verified over and over again. Paul thanked God that when the Thessalonians heard from the missionaries "the word of God . . . you accepted it not as the word of men but as what it really is, the word of God" (1 Thes

2:13). They did so because "our gospel came to you not only in word, but also in power and in the Holy Spirit and with full conviction" (1:5). It is always so in renewal times. God's message—the gospel call to repentance, faith, and holiness, to praise and prayer, witness and worship—authenticates itself unambiguously to men's consciences, and there is no room for half measures in response. That leads to our next point.

(3)Sensitiveness to sin. Deep awareness of what things are sinful and how sinful we ourselves are—*conviction* of sin, to use the old phrase—is the third phenomenon of renewal that calls for notice. No upsurge of religious interest or excitement merits the name of renewal if there is no deep sense of sin at its heart. God's coming, and the consequent impact of his word, makes Christians much more sensitive to sin than they previously were: consciences become tender and a profound humbling takes place. The gospel of forgiveness through Christ's cross comes to be loved as never before, when folk see their need of it so much

more clearly. That conviction of sin was very much part of the early Christian story, and the opening chapters of Acts give us three examples of it.

In Acts 2:37-41 we see conviction *accepted*. Peter's congregation was "pierced to the heart" (2:37) with a sense of their guilt for Jesus' death. The Greek word for "pierced" means literally to inflict a violent blow; it is a painfully vivid image for what was an acutely painful experience. Shattered, the congregation cried out, "Brethren, what shall we do?" Peter showed them the way of faith, repentance, and discipleship, and three thousand of them took it. Thus, conviction was the means of their blessing.

In Acts 7:54-60 we see conviction *resisted*. Stephen has accused his Jewish judges of resisting the Spirit, murdering the Christ, and showing contempt for the law (7:51-53). They are "cut to the quick" (7:54)—the Greek word literally means "sawn apart"; it expresses the inner turmoil arising from the conjunction of inescapable guilt and uncontrollable anger. Too proud to admit they had been wrong, they ground their teeth, yelled at Stephen, stopped their ears, mobbed him, ran him out of town, and stoned him to death. The trauma of felt guilt had driven them into hysteria. Conviction in this case was the means of their hardening.

Then in Acts 5:1-10 we see conviction *killing*—literally. Peter tells Ananias that he has lied to the Holy Spirit and to God, and Ananias dies. A divine judgment, certainly; but what account of it should we give in human terms? The most natural view is that in that revitalized community, where sensitiveness to the presence of God and hence to the foulness of sin was exceedingly strong, the realization of what he had done so overwhelmed Ananias that his frame could not stand it, and he died of shock; and Sapphira the same. They literally could not live with their sin. Thus, conviction became the means of their judgment.

What do we learn from this? That under revival conditions consciences are so quickened that conviction of sin becomes strong and terrible, inducing agonies of mind that are beyond imagining till they happen. But conviction of sin is a means, not an end; the Spirit of God convinces of sin in order to induce repentance, and one of the more striking features of renewal movements is the depth of repentance into which both saints and sinners are led. Repentance, as we know, is basically not moaning and remorse, but turning and change: "about turn, quick march" is a good formula to express its meaning. In 2 Corinthians 7:10, Paul says, "The sorrow that is according to the will of God produces a repentance without regret, leading to salvation," and in the next verse he applauds the robustness of the Corinthians' repentance in the matter about which he had rebuked them. "What earnestness . . . this godly sorrow has produced in you: what vindication of yourselves, what indignation, what fear, what longing, what zeal, what avenging of wrong!" Vivid conviction produces vigorous repentance.

In times of renewal the impulse constantly recurs, often in defiance of cultural conditioning, to signalize and seal one's repentance by public confession of what one is renouncing: as was done at Ephesus, apparently spontaneously, when "many . . . of those who had believed kept coming, confessing and disclosing their practices" (Acts 19:18), and some occult practitioners went so far as publicly to burn their very valuable books of spells—a costly and humbling gesture, no doubt, but equally certainly a liberating one for those who made it. One or more of three motives prompts public confession. It is partly for *purgation*: individuals feel that the only way to get evil things off their conscience and out of their lives is by renouncing them publicly. Sins are also confessed for *healing* (Jas 5:16): pocketing pride and admitting one's faults and failings to others is part of God's therapy. And, finally, sins are confessed for *doxology*: "Come and hear, all who fear God, and I will tell of what He has done for my soul" (Ps 66:16). This kind of confession is likely to appear spontaneously wherever there is genuine renewal.

(4) Liveliness in community. Love and generosity, unity and joy, assurance and

boldness, a spirit of praise and prayer, and a passion to reach out to win others are recurring marks of renewed communities. So is divine power in their preachers, a power which has nothing to do with natural eloquence. John Howe, the Puritan, once Cromwell's chaplain, spoke of this in a passage in a sermon on Ezekiel 39:29 ("I have poured out my Spirit upon the house of Israel, saith the Lord God"). Preaching in 1678 and looking back on the great days of the Puritan revival under the Commonwealth, he told his congregation:

When the Spirit shall be poured forth plentifully ... I believe you will hear much other kind of sermons ... than you are wont to do now-a-days. ... It is plain, too sadly plain, that there is a great retraction of the Spirit of God even from us. We [preachers] know not how to speak living sense [*sensus*, a feeling, felt reality] unto souls, how to get within you; our words die in our mouths, or drop and die between you and us. We even faint, when we speak; long experienced

unsuccessfulness makes us despond.
We speak not as persons that hope to
prevail, that expect to make you more
serious, heavenly, mindful of God, and
to walk more like Christians. . . . When
such an effusion of the Spirit shall be
as is here signified . . . ministers . . .
shall know how to speak to better
purpose, with more compassion and
sense, with more seriousness, with
more authority and allurement, than
we now find we can.[7]

Also in renewal times God acts quickly:
his work accelerates. When Paul left
Thessalonika after between two and three
weeks' ministry there he left behind him a
virile church whose quality can be gauged
from 1 Thessalonians 1-3. God had moved
fast. No wonder Paul asks them to pray
that "the word of the Lord may speed on
[literally, run] and triumph, as it did
among you" (2 Thes 3:1). Truth spreads,
and people are born again and grow in
Christ, with amazing rapidity under
renewal conditions.

(5) Fruitfulness in testimony. Revival of
the church always has an evangelistic

and ethical overspill into the world: Christians proclaim by word and deed the power of the new life, souls are won, and a community conscience informed by Christian values emerges.

Such in outline is the constant pattern by which genuine movements of renewal identify themselves. Christians in renewal are accordingly found living in God's presence (*coram Deo*), attending to his word, feeling acute concern about sin and righteousness, rejoicing in the assurance of Christ's love and their own salvation, spontaneously constant in worship, and tirelessly active in witness and service, fueling these activities by praise and prayer. The question that presses, therefore, is not whether renewal is approved as a theological idea or claimed as a shibboleth of fashion (to say "we are in renewal" is almost mandatory in some circles nowadays!). The question that presses is whether renewal is actually displayed in the lives of Christian individuals and communities: whether this quality of Christian life is there or not. Which brings us to our final section.

The Quest for Renewal

This is where analysis finally merges into application. I have three points to develop: First, our guilt in not being renewed, and God's call to us to repent of it; second, our inability to renew ourselves, and God's call to us to seek renewal from him; third, our obligation to remove obstacles to our being renewed, and God's call to us to act now in this matter. What this amounts to is a summons to us all to be more honest with God, more simple and thoroughgoing in our response to his grace, more open and straightforward both with him and with others, than we may have been hitherto. Let me try to spell this out as I understand it.

Theme one: our guilt in not being renewed, and God's call to us to repent of it. For this I need only refer you once more to the letters of our Lord to the seven churches of the Revelation. With only one of them, the Philadelphian congregation, was the Savior pleased; the Ephesian church was condemned for having left its first love (2:4f), the church at Sardis for being dead (3:1), and the church at Laodicia for being self-satisfied and self-deceived. "I know your works," says Jesus to them; "you are neither cold nor hot. Would that you were cold or hot! So, because you are lukewarm, and neither cold nor hot, I will spew you out of my mouth. For you say, I am rich, I have prospered, and I need nothing; not knowing that you are wretched, pitiable, poor, blind, and naked. . . . Those whom I love I rebuke and chasten; so be zealous and repent" (3:15-17, 19). It is hard to doubt that this is the mind of Jesus with regard to many churches in North America today.

Biblical theology knows no middle condition, for churches or for Christians, between spiritual advance under God's blessing and spiritual decline under his displeasure. The root of spiritual decline is always human unfaithfulness in some form, and its fruit is always chastening judgment from God, whose gracious plan and supernatural enabling are hereby slighted and dishonored. Marks of decline include high tolerance of half-heartedness, moral failure, and compromise; low expectations of holiness in oneself and others; willingness to remain Christian pygmies; apathy about the advancement of God's cause and his glory; and contentment, even complacency, with things as they are. Charles Finney once said, "Christians are more to blame for not being revived, than sinners are for not being converted."[8] Was he right? It is, at the very least, a question worth thinking about as we reflect on the relevance to ourselves of Jesus' words to the Laodiceans. And perhaps in doing this we shall need to make our own the words of the Anglican litany: "from hardness of heart, and contempt of thy word and commandment, good Lord, deliver us."

So we move to theme two: our inability to renew ourselves, and our need to seek this blessing from God by prayer. The point here is that whereas self-reliance is natural (we might almost say, instinctive) to us in our fallenness, it is beyond us to initiate spiritual renewal by any form of activity that we organize. The principle is the same as that underlying Isaiah 22:8-14, where Judah's feverish bustle of defensive activity in face of trouble was ruling out anything in the nature of a genuine return to God and a genuine dependence on him for the deliverance which only he could give. To look to human ingenuity, however, for that which only God in his grace can give is arrogant, inept, and in the outcome barren. And that is how it is in the matter of renewal. When Christians, by the Laodicean character of their lives and their ecclesiastical systems, have quenched the fire of God's Spirit, and so brought about a withdrawal of God's presence and glory, it is beyond their power to kindle the fire again, much as they might wish to do so; only God himself, by his own quickening visitation, can renew, and for this we have to wait on him in patient, persistent, penitent prayer until he is pleased to act. Charles Finney, who for a decade after his conversion was used by God in a continuous revival ministry, came to think, evidently generalizing from that experience, that self-examination and earnest prayer on a congregation's part would always secure a divine visitation and fresh outpouring of the Spirit immediately. But the experience of many who have sought to implement this formula, and indeed the different and disappointing experience of Finney himself in later years, shows that this is not so. In no situation can revival be infallibly predicted or precipitated; there are no natural laws of renewal for man the manager to discover and exploit. That, however, is no cause for discouragement, for the other side of the coin is that the possibility of renewal can never be precluded either; no one can set limits to the graciousness of God who has promised that we shall find him when we seek him with all our hearts. To seek God and his renewing grace, recognizing that he can renew us though we cannot renew ourselves, is in this instance the only constructive thing that is open to us to do. "Ask, and it will be given you; seek, and you will find," says our Lord (Mt 7:7). The Psalter provides several pattern prayers for this purpose, notably Psalms 44, 67, 74, 79, and 85. Waiting on God in constant acknowledgment of need, pleading that he should move in mercy, is the way forward here.

Finally, we move to theme three: our obligation to remove hindrances to renewal, and God's call to us to begin doing this now. A moment ago I said that we cannot precipitate a visitation from God. That is true; God is sovereign in these matters and takes action to answer prayer at his own speed and in his own good time. Yet there is something we can do at this present moment to bring spiritual quickening nearer, and that is to break with things that are in their own nature Spirit-quenching.

For instance: surely *clericalism* as a leadership style is Spirit-quenching. Clericalism, which on my analysis involves more persons than the ordained, is a sort of conspiracy between leaders and those led: the one party (it does not matter which) says, "all spiritual ministry should be left to the leader," and the other party says, "yes, that's right." Some leaders embrace clericalism because it gives them power; others, running scared, embrace it because they fear lest folk ministering alongside them should overshadow them, or because they feel incapable of handling an every-member-ministry situation. But every-member-ministry in the body of Christ is the New Testament pattern, and anything which obstructs or restricts it is an obstacle to a renewing visitation from God. What does this suggest that leaders, and others, ought to do now?

Again: surely *formalism* as a worship style is Spirit-quenching. But many churches seem to view worship in a way that can only be called formalistic, for their interest is limited to performing set routines with suitable correctness, and there is no apparent desire on anyone's part actually to meet God. What does this suggest that leaders, and others, ought to do now?

Yet once more: surely personal attitudes of *complacency* about things as they are is Spirit-quenching. Think of your own church or fellowship: to what extent do you see in it the reality of worship? faith? repentance? knowledge? holiness? Do its members resolutely, energetically, passionately love the Lord? Do they love each other? How do they pray? How do they give? How much support do they get from each other in times of personal need? How much sharing of their faith do they do, or try to do? Ought you to be content with things as they are? Think also of yourself, and of what these folk see in you. Ought either they or you to be content with what you are? It must be expected that those led will become like their leaders; that is the natural thing to happen; but if it happens so in your church or fellowship, will that be good enough? What does this line of thought suggest that leaders, and others, ought to do now?

The first step, perhaps, to the renewal of the Christian people is that leaders should begin to repent of their too-ready acceptance of too-low levels of attainment both in themselves and in those whom they lead, and should learn to pray from their hearts the simple-sounding but totally demanding prayer in Edwin Orr's chorus: *"send a revival—start the work in me."* The second step, perhaps, is for leaders to challenge their followers as to whether they are not too much like the Laodiceans of Revelation, and whether Jesus' searing words to these latter—"you are lukewarm. . . . you say, I am rich, I have prospered, and I need nothing; not knowing that you are wretched, pitiable, poor, blind, and naked. . . . be zealous and repent. Behold, I stand at the door and knock. . . ."—do not apply directly to themselves, here and now. The third step, perhaps, is for us all, leaders and led together, to become more serious, expectant, and honest with each other as we look to God in our use of the means of grace—sermon and sacrament, worship and witness, praise and prayer, meditation and petition—and as we seek to make our own the psalmist's plea: "Search me, O God, and know my heart! Try me and know my thoughts! And see if there be any wicked way in me, and lead me in the way everlasting!" (Ps 139:23-24). Then the fourth step, perhaps, will be to trust the Holy Spirit to lead us on from there.

Does this prospect strike awe into you? I am sure that it does, and it has the same effect on me. But that is no justification for drawing back from it, when our need of it is so plain.

"O Lord, I have heard the report of thee, and thy work, O Lord, do I fear. In the midst of the years renew it; in the midst of the years make it known; in wrath remember mercy" (Hab 3:2).

Let all the people say: amen.

Notes

1. Quoted from T.H.L. Parker, *The Oracles of God: An Introduction to the Preaching of John Calvin* (London: Lutterworth Press, 1947), p. 60.
2. Note especially the pioneer studies by J. Edwin Orr of post-Methodist awakenings: *The Second Evangelical Awakening in Britain* (London: Marshall, Morgan & Scott, 1949); *The Second Evangelical Awakening in America* (Grand Rapids, Mich.: Zondervan, 1952); *The Fervent Prayer: The World Wide Impact of the Great Awakening of 1858* (Chicago: Moody Press, 1974) (all three dealing with the movement of 1957-60); *The Eager Feet: Evangelical Awakenings, 1790-1830* (Chicago: Moody Press, 1975); *The Flaming Tongue: Evangelical Awakenings, 1900-1910* (Chicago: Moody Press, 2nd ed., 1975); *The Light of the Nations: Evangelical Renewal and Advance in the Nineteenth Century* (Exeter: Paternoster Press and Grand Rapids: Eerdmans, 1965); *Campus Aflame: Evangelical Awakenings in College Communities* (Glendale, Calif.: Regal Books, 1971); *Evangelical Awakenings in Southern Asia* (Minneapolis,

Minn.: Bethany Fellowship, 1975); *Evangelical Awakenings in Africa* (Minneapolis: Bethany Fellowship, 1975); *Evangelical Awakenings in the South Seas* (Minneapolis: Bethany Fellowship, 1976). Note also J.T. Carson, *God's River in Spate* (Presbyterian Church of Ireland, 1958; on the Irish revival of 1859); J. Goforth, *By My Spirit* (Grand Rapids, Mich.: Zondervan, 1967; on the Chinese revivals of 1908); E. Eifion Evans, *When He Is Come* (Bridgend, Wales: Evangelical Press of Wales; 2nd ed., 1967; on the Welsh revival of 1859); and *The Welsh Revival of 1904* (Bridgend, Wales: Evangelical Press of Wales, 1969).

3. Richard F. Lovelace, *Dynamics of Spiritual Life* (Downer's Gróve, Ill.: InterVarsity Press, 1979), pp. 21f.

4. *Ibid.*, especially chapter 2. See also the same author's *Renewal as a Way of Life* (Downer's Grove, Ill.: InterVarsity Press, 1985).

5. Arthur Wallis, *In the Day of Thy Power* (London: Christian Literature Crusade, 1956), p. 20.

6. Duncan Campbell, *The Lewis Awakening 1949-1953* (Edinburgh: Faith Mission, 1954), p. 29.

7. John Howe, *Works* (London: F. Westley and A.H. Davis, 1832), p. 575.

8. Charles G. Finney, *Revivals of Religion* (London: Oliphants, 1928), p. 20

Other Titles in the Christian Essentials Series

True Confessions
Owning Up to the Secret Everybody Knows
Philip Yancey

In *True Confessions* Philip Yancey asks the question, "Whatever became of sin?" With personal examples, he points out that life with God involves taking responsibility for our wrongdoing and trusting in the love of God for forgiveness.

To Live or Die
Facing Decisions at the End of Life
C. Everett Koop, M.D.

Dr. Koop explores the complex issues surrounding death and dying and offers a Christian approach to making decisions, for oneself and others.

Women: the Challenge and the Call
An Agenda for Christian Women in Today's World
Dee Jepsen

It is time for both men and women to understand the vital importance of a woman's contributions in the church and in society. Dee Jepsen calls women to assert themselves against the forces that threaten to destroy family life— widespread pornography, the erosion of respect for human life, and the pursuit of selfishness.

Word (UK) Ltd.
9 Holdom Avenue,
Bletchley, Milton Keynes